FROM
PRISON
TO *Poetry*

FROM
PRISON
TO *Poetry*

RICKEY O. QUINN

FROM PRISON TO POETRY

iUniverse books may be ordered through booksellers or by contacting:

iUniverse
1663 Liberty Drive
Bloomington, IN 47403
www.iuniverse.com
1-800-Authors (1-800-288-4677)

ISBN: 978-1-5320-9123-0 (sc)
ISBN: 978-1-5320-9124-7 (e)

Print information available on the last page.

iUniverse rev. date: 12/17/2019

DEDICATION

The dedication of this book is to my Lord and Savior, Jesus Christ, whom I'm giving my gift back to, along with the nation of believers of God the Father, God the Son, and God the Holy Spirit. Additionally, I want to dedicate this book first to my children: Angel Quin, Siedha Quinn, Qeletha Smith, Demetrius Quinn, and Antonio Felton. Thanking my family and friends that encouraged me along the way. Thanks to all of you!

CONTENTS

𝒯HE LIFE, THE EPISTLE

◄O►

I knew you before you entered your mother's womb, I also knew your life, I'd have to groom. And so it began, my world of sin, so get in where you fit in. September 1959, it was my time, the whole truth and I'm not lying.

From Greenville, Mississippi, to Indianola, Mississippi, "Mrs. Quinn, will you keep my baby for two weeks?" That's what my mother asked or told my grandma. My grandma agreed because she knew I was in need. Somehow or another grandma believed, never once thinking that I was a bad seed, but an infant child in need indeed.

On buttermilk and bananas was my daily nutrition. This was prescribed by my mother's physician. I was born bowlegged, and I had diarrhea real bad, but that was nothing to Grandma because old folks' remedies was what she had.

Now time went and time came... where's my mother? And was I the one to blame? Then one day, just out of the blue, my grandma's door opened, guess who walked through, my mama looking all fresh and brand new.

"Oh! Mrs. Quinn," my mother replied, "I thought upon my return my baby would have died." Grandma looked at her and then she said, "Dead! Not that I'm afraid or that I'm scared, but that's a burden for your own heart and head."

Grandma said it was three months exact before my mother came back. Grandma and Granddaddy were feeding me more of that Similac. I was filling out and getting real fat.

Now grandma and granddaddy were a very hard working couple, and they were, of course, great intimate lovers. Now this was proven by my dad and his three brothers, Willie Lee, Leroy, and Levi, along with my dad.

These are the men that was on my side. They were wise, had lots of pride, and their families were never denied. Granddaddy was the king for us all. He had big dreams and things. I can remember, when we had two stores and a service station. But for me they were pure temptation.

I'd try to steal from granddaddy's store, but after I got caught, I wouldn't steal anymore. See granddaddy had a firm hand that he would land and make you understand that he was most definitely the man.

Now my uncle Willie Lee was the baby boy. He'd do things that he liked and most of the time they were for fun and joy. He'd drink a little wine and whisky sometimes, but never in his life did he participate in crimes.

Now my uncle Leroy lived his life on a somewhat different but clever lever. I looked up to him regardless to whether he would be the one to persuade me to always do better. He was a go-getter, nowhere near being a quitter.

I can remember when granddaddy had passed away. I did what I wanted regardless to what grandma would say. But on this particular day, oh how can I forget, Grandma told my uncle Leroy that I had lost my respect.

I hadn't really done anything that I thought was so bad or wrong, even though when the street lights came on, I should have been at home. And this wasn't the first time, this went on, and on and on.

My dear granny had took all that she could take. It was now time for discipline and nowhere to escape. My uncle whipped my ass till it broke like glass. I tried hiding underneath the bed. I was dead, scared, I cry out, I begged, but to no avail. And if that happened today, you would go straight to jail. And if God was the judge, you would go straight to hell.

After he finished whipping my behind, he had a tub of bath water that also helped me get back in line. After that, he moved to Chicago and didn't have to worry about me anymore.

Now, my other uncle he was just too cool, smooth and slow to move. He basically played by truth and, of course, God's rules. And, believe me, he wasn't nobody's fool.

Yeah, I remember when he had to twist my cap, and I'm not talking about me getting across his lap. That's right, he whipped my ass because I was something bad, and I thought I could have whatever the world had.

I remember wanting for Christmas a batman suit, and when I didn't get it, my ass became a Christmas tribute. Today, I understand why they were really in my life. One was because they loved me, two was to help me do right, act right, be right.

During all that talking about my life and trouble, where's my mother before I go any further? Time has come and time has gone. The Quinn's family is where I belong, and, of course, where I call home.

From grade school to high school, I thought I was cool. But one thing for sure, education to me was no fool. I played the trumpet in the high school band, and today I'm sure that I still can.

Baseball was my game. I played so well until I thought it would end in the Hall of Fame. Well school was cool, but after high school what would I choose?

The United States Army was my final thought. I had to do something before my life became naught. So I joined the Army to be all I could be. But I really did it to find my destiny.

I had a son that was born. I needed money, I was torn. So they sent me to Germany. That's where I was stationed. I immediately caught a case that didn't carry probation.

Now that was stupid because right around that time came my oldest daughter, "Cupid." I fought the case with God's mercy and grace. I knew my life had become a total waste because, in the joint, life was what I was facing.

My uncles got me a German lawyer for my support. I was found guilty in a German court, thousands of miles away from my family and home. I was in trouble. I was alone and grown.

To be continued...

STEPS

Steps in life that I made myself
Steps I made without anyone's help
Steps that lead me through a dangerous life
Steps that I now think about twice
Steps that I now know I should have kept
Steps like these cannot help.
Steps for profit, fame and gain,
Steps not walking but running the fast lanes.
Steps that hurt your family and friend,
Steps that bring life to a complete end.
Steps that gave me the "slick Rick" name,
Steps that cause me to live my life in vain.
Steps that speaks to your heart and mind,
Steps of darkness where the sun doesn't
shine.
But there are steps that can be made slow,
God gives them and the way we should go.
Walking with God in His love and affection,
Because He is the map to all of our direction.
Steps that show you all the dangerous routes,
Steps bring us in but never get us out.
Steps that give us an everyday payday,
Steps that never show us the life of God's
tollway.

$\mathcal{A}$ PRAYER OF THANKS

Lord, I want to thank You for who You are
and for what
You've done for me,
You're the only one that makes my life
complete.
When I'm down and feeling depressed, You
pick me up
and bless my less, letting me know, that this
is only a test.
You watch over me, during my sleep and
slumber,
changing my attitude, and I'm now humble.
You were there for me when everyone else
had left,
You gave me confidence to believe in You and
myself.
You've stayed the hands of death, hurt, harm,
and danger,
You've blessed me more than any friend or
stranger.
How can I repay You for all You've done for
me?
I know You don't ask for much, "just a closer
walk with Thee."
So be that light in my life so when I'm in
darkness,
You'll shine bright.

Set me free from that which is not like Thee,
save me that I'll be with You in the heavenly.
Thank You for your patience, and not instant
gratification,
Thank You much for our personal relation.

𝒜 FRIEND IN DEED

—◦—

You've been in my life for quite some time,
and I admire you as a true friend of mine.
I've been through much with no one to care,
but together we tried
side by side.

Together we shared because you were always
there,
you were there ready and willing, with time
and patience, to fill my feeling.
There's so many good things I could say about
you, that's true in what
in what you do.

A heart of gold that can't be bought or sold,
God's given and it can't be controlled.
You're just you, a friend in deed,
you're so special to me, the friend that I need.

And I pray to God that your heart remains
whole,
and the quality of your life will maintain
God's goals.
And there's no secret hidden within you,
you're very special and your heart is true.

Friends like you are far and few,
friends like you make life anew,
friends like you are okay,
a friend like you can't be found every day.

Thanks again for being my personal friend.

𝒜 PRIZE TO RECOGNIZE

◄◦►

Your eyes are as bright as the morning sun,
and your relentless personality tells me that
you're the one.
I really don't know much about you,
I'm believing in my heart that you are true.

I'm just a brother that don't like trouble,
I stand alone and not with others,
I'm not a player,
and nowhere near being gullible.

I find in my mind that you are as sweet as red
table wine,
you're my kind, and I just want to spend with
you some quality time.
I believe, I'm convinced,
that you are the one, you're God sent.

I'm deeply sorrowful for your mishaps in life,
but with me, I'll treat you right, day and
night,
keep this relationship tight,
where we won't argue, fuss or fight.
And of course take it to levels of spiritual and
romantic heights
and delights.

See my time can be your time and yours
mine,
I'm talking genuine, divine time,
that together, you and I, we'll shine,
and future time of you being all mine.

Let me say that you're the queen that
enlightens my everything,
my every dream,
you're the soul that God has redeemed,
I just want to play on your team.

Can this be over? This nightmare, not my
dream,
you being my queen and I'm your king,
together we'll accomplish and share
everything,
we can even share the same genes.

You're that woman of every side,
that's why you're special
and I'm glad I recognize.

$\mathcal{A}$S IT IS WRITTEN

—◦—

I'm locked in and not out,
faith to believe and not doubt.
You've told me time and time again just what
you wanted me to do,
I wouldn't take heed, so everything fell
through.

I know You sit high and look low,
a fool I am because I know the way to go.
God, I ask for Your divine forgiveness,
knowing all the time You don't have to hear
this.

I've acknowledged my mistakes, present and
past,
but through Your mercy and grace, this far
I've last.
Help me, please, I pray of Thee,
that Your wrath, of course, doesn't fall on me.

Giving You the reverence that You so deserve,
thanking You much for my life You've
reserved,
because You could have kicked me to the
curve.

Bless my heart that it is pure,
and my ongoing decision is positive and sure.
Salvation with You, I will truly endure,
because there's no sickness that You can't
cure.

Guide me through the dos that I didn't,
so my life will be an example,
as it is written.

A WOMAN OF WISDOM

◄○►

God has blessed you through these many
years,
through trials and tribulations and your many
ordeals.
It's okay, if I must say, God has a special
blessing
coming your way.

Out of all the good work that you've put in
it's not in vain, you'll see it again.
Things you've said and encouraged me to do,
I knew they were true, coming from a woman
like you.

God has blessed you with unspeakable
wisdom, too, of course,
helping me in making Godly decisions,
thank you for your sweetness and being so
nice,
thank you, mother, for all of your advice.

Thanks again for who you are and for what
you stand for
and I pray that God will bless you with some
more.

LOVE YOU ALWAYS

$\mathscr{A}$ BUSINESS PRAYER

—◄o►—

Bless this business that it may prosper and
grow,
bless all my consumers, where they'll know
this
here business is the place to be and, of course,
the place to go.

Bless their hearts as well as their minds,
that they will return at any given time.
Bless this business and the service that we
render,
that we, of course, our customers will
remember.

Lord, bless us all that we don't fall,
and we will give Your people our all and all,
where we will beat, defeat, right the wrong
and
they will return because this is where they
belong.

So when you leave our place of business,
tell a friend where you've been,
and you're sure that you'll be
coming back again.

$\mathcal{B}$LESSED

—◄o►—

Life has given me truly a fair shake,
it's proven daily, when I'm allowed to awake.
I can't complain, my life is somewhat blank,
for you, Lord, I have nothing but thanks.

He's blessed me with things that mean
nothing to Him,
He's blessed me with my family and then He
bless them.
I ask for material dreams that really didn't
mean a thing.
but God Being God, He had to bless my heart.
He gave me a vision and, of course, lots of
wisdom,
I even ask for wealth, for me and someone
else,
He said, "I gave you wisdom,
so get your wealth yourself."

Oh, I love Him dearly, He lends an ear to hear
me,
so heaven is now my goal, my life He now
controls,
He lifts my every burden, my mind may up
for certain.

I'll praise His holy name, because Satan plays
nothing but games,
I'm tired of running from Satan, this time I'll
be waiting.
I know he's going to attack,
but with God's Word I'll fight back.

See, I've got to be ready, mind, body and soul,
I'm going to be raptured up,
and I'm going to be made whole.

$\mathcal{B}$ LACK WOMAN

—◦—

They say women like you come a dime a
dozen,
trashy and flashy, talking about you, they
wasn't
because the quality that you give makes life
more real,
it's more than sex or any sex thrill that gives a
man
chills, make him pay bills, without making
dealing,
this is his freewill, and that's for real for real.

See, you're a rose, that I've chose, and when
the wind blows
you're in the nose of those that goes and
glows, you make
life grows.

You're sweeter than honey, richer than
money, and the remainder
of your days will be blessed and sunny.

Finer than silk, shinier than gold, this is what
I know not what
I was told.

And your personality is a definitely with or
without me,
I'm sure you agree.

But together we'll shine because I'm yours
and you're mine, divine
and I isn't lying; you're fine, and I came in
your life at God's appointed
time, not mine.

I've dealt with women on each corner of the
world, but I'll have you to know
that you are a giant in a midget's world, girl.
So how can I compare you to any woman out
there?
I can't I swear, where?

A woman like you comes very rare, and I
declare you're fair,
you're my prayer.

And there's one more thing that I thought you
should know,
you're so unique, sweet and i admire all the
negativism that you put and keep
underneath your feet.

Listen, it's not your booty, nor is it your
beauty, but it's what inside
that makes you a cutie.

So, black woman, talk is cheap and with you
it's beneath, so stay sweet
because God made you whole as well as
complete.

YOU'RE THAT DREAM THAT I'VE SEEN
SOMEWHERE, IN VOGUE
OR EBONY MAGAZINE, BLACK WOMAN,
YOU'RE MY NUBIAN QUEEN.

$\mathcal{B}$ LACKMAN

Do you not understand, that you're the man
and you can,
with your mind and not your hands?
Did you not know that you're in demand, and
you can possess
the fruits of God's land with a plan?
Do you understand what I'm saying
BLACKMAN?
Well, in your heart, you're part of God's
divine plan.

BLACKMAN, isn't it bizarre, how you get so
far and know not
who you really are. Yeah, that is bizarre.
You're a gift from God, you're smart, but
everything you do is
hard, because you don't play your cards,
they're in your heart.

BLACKMAN, will you listen?
Because you be missing and resisting and
God be insisting, then
you two become distance, now you're right
back to for instance.
See it's time to stop hanging and slanging,
negative acquainting
and start God song-sanging.

BLACKMAN, you have not because you ask
not, and when you get
notice it's not a lot, but you're content with
just what you got.
See it's the prototype, that's right, divine
light, that's forever bright,
that holds life tight, but you got to have
insight.

See, this is milk and honey, let's not even
mention the money.
BLACKMAN, BLACKMAN,
it's time for interacting, because you be
slacking, think you facting,
ghetto macking, God's people attacking,
mouth yakking, never
relaxing, you be whacking, BLACKMAN.
Let's just say we will call those things that are
not as though they were
and watch the manifestation of God as they
do occur.

BLACKMAN, BLACKMAN, DO YOU REALLY
UNDERSTAND,
BLACKMAN?

CONGRATULATIONS

Now that you have achieved it, my mind and
heart,
always did believe it,
so your time has come, for you to receive it.

I didn't have any doubt, because I knew what you
were about.

Long hours and hard work, even during the times
when your head would hurt.

The best is yet to come, keep your head up,
never forgetting where you come from.

See, I knew you had great potentials, it shows
today
earned credentials.

Now this one level, that'll take you to the next, it
might
seemed hard, but I guarantee, you'll never

regret, forget, be disrespected, because you're in
that
position to do nothing but collect.

SO ALWAYS REMEMBER, THE MORE YOU
KNOW
THE MORE YOU GROW, AND THAT'S
UNIVERSAL.

*D*EAR MAMA

—◄o►—

Words can't explain, neither can they express.
the smiles in my heart because of your
happiness.

From the time that I can remember, back in
the days,
your voice I would hear, "Children, give God
His praise."

Sundays were special, and we all went to
church, but
every time we did wrong, our behinds you'd
hurt.

Beans, greens, cornbread was basically all
that we ate,
but one thing you taught us and that was not
to hate.

Mama, I love you with whole heart and soul,
thanks for everything,
including helping me achieving my goals,
no greater love can one give to their kids, and
if there was,
God Almighty forbids,

Mama, all I can give is love in return, thanks
mama for your greatest
Concern.

LOVE YOU ALWAYS

$\mathcal{D}$ISGUISED

‹o›

Isn't it crazy, better yet, it amazes me, how
they betrayed me,
and think it doesn't faze me.
So I took a good look, 'cause I was shook,
from what was said
and from what I'd read in their history book.
So I began to pray, because in reality, prayer
was the only way.
So I kneeled, knowing that my faith was
sealed, or to see if it
was the Lord's will because the truth had to
be revealed.

Our eyes are open wide and we don't even
see, what's about to
happen shouldn't be no mystery.
See they took the land from the man, they
took the reservation,
and without any confrontation or
explanation, the reservation
became the plantation.

For nights and days they thought of ways to
name this country,
the free and the brave, which was built by our
ancestors, Negro
slaves, that worked so hard and was never
paid, this they did until

their dying days.
Now these are the people that paved the way.
After all the years,
tears, and fears, not to forget the sweat and
neglect, we still don't
have any respect.
Where's our retribution to a common
solution? Why isn't that in the
Constitution? See, we don't want to be
praised, neither do we want God's
glory, we just want to get paid and not played,
then rewrite
the story.
But that'll never be because the system was
designed stunt our
growth and to steal our identity.
Our eyes are open wide and we don't even
see, what's about to
happen shouldn't be know mystery.
Now here's a sample or shall I say example of
what America is about
to taste, they're here to destroy the whole
human race.
So we got to find a place that's safe, where we
can embrace, for once
face to face, and that place is in God's mercy
and God's grace.

This is the beginning of today's sorrow, but
what's to come, could
be tomorrow's horror.
The beast has been released and they say he's

from the Middle East,
And he's here in America to have a feast, and
leave all humanity with
no peace and plenty deceased.

𝓕AITH

—◆—

Sometimes in life, sickness comes upon us
that we don't
think is right,
but God is in control, He'll fight the fight.

Jesus said cast your cares upon him for the
careth for you.
And I want you to know that I careth too.

Not understanding the hurting pains in your
mortal body
and finite mind
I encourage you to know that after the rain
comes God's
sunshine.

I hope you can understand exactly what I
mean, I'm talking
about the substance of things hoped for and
the evidence of
things not seen

and even-though, you think your prayers go
unheard, well I've got
news for you, through Jesus, God hears every
word.

FORGIVE ME, I APOLOGIZE

—◄○►—

My heart keeps telling me to do the right
things,
and if I don't, I can't fulfill none of my
dreams.
So in order for me to arise and my differences
set aside,
my heart tells me to apologize.

Because God knows, I'm sick and tired of
being sick and tired.
Tired of the lies, alibis, pride and all the
positivism I sometimes
denies.

But with a clean heart, clear mind, which is
food for the soul,
life becomes beautiful, and God knows it
grows and grows,
and grows.

You know sometimes we do things, say
things, or think things out
of context, to people we care for, then we lose
their respect.
But I know that you know that what I'm
saying is truth, and it's nothing
new, we were taught this as youths.

But this is based on forgiving and living, and
how we should be as
men and women.

So the thing to do, forgive and apply, because
the same thing that
makes you laugh makes you cry.

We're not perfect, and we're going to make
mistakes, but it's imperative
to forgive, if we are to grow in God's Heavenly
grace.
Last but not least, this I must release, we
must forgive and be at peace
So if we live by the sword, we must definitely
die by the sword.

So now you know it, coming from a true poet,
take the seed, show it,
and God will truly bless you, that's if you sow
it.

*F*REE AT LAST

—◄◦►—

Time is out for me using and abusing, always
excusing, losing,
never rightfully choosing, so from this point
on, I'm refusing.
Questioning myself, "Who am I?" and "Where
am I from?"

Because what I was doing wasn't smart but
straight-up super dumb,
so I've repented, till Jesus comes.

No more I'll gain, playing games, short
changing my brain, and
Other stupid things, being in pain, with no
one to blame, "I was
insane but my remains are godly change.

I'd use the "gift of gab," to reach out and grab,
and at the end of
the day, I still wouldn't have
you know, dipping and dabbing and not
having.

So today and every day "Christ Jesus, I trust,"
it's mandatory it's a
must, it's a plus, because He died for us.

Believe it if you want to, because if you don't
I'm going to, I refuse to
live like I did before, you know, living low,
can't grow knowing
not which way to go.

And I understand that people are going to
talk about my past, but that's okay, I
don't care, I'm free, I'm free at last.

You can talk about me, 'til you're blue in the
face, but it's not about me, it's
about God's mercy and grace.

I remember not the bad in my past, all I
remember now is that I'm
free, I'm free at last.

$\mathcal{F}$ROM ME TO YOU

---◦---

Memories of you, memories so sweet, vivid,
and true,
memories in my mind, and you don't even
have a clue.
These are memories of me and you, this is
what I'll do,

I'll travel the orbits, which is very far, this I'll
do because
of who you are.
I'll allow no limitations or negative
information to come
between God's beautiful creation.

I speak these words because they are truth
and nothing
or no one can cut or break loose.

See, you're my clothes, when I'm cold, you got
hooks in
my nose but I don't mind, I've been exposed,
to the high and the lows,
you got me froze when you pose and those,

you're my strength, you're God sent, for you
I'm weak,
can I rub your feet?

Whisper in your ear until you fall asleep.
I'll do these things and of course many more,
maybe I'm
moving too fast, allow me to take this slow, so
I can see
you glow, from your head to your pinky toe,
and even though
no one has to know, when we close the door,
and love
begins to grow like never before.

See we don't blame, but remain sane, and free
from pain and
playing games.

SO WITH YOUR PERMISSION, WE'RE ON
A MISSION,
SO DEFINE THE DEFINITION, BECAUSE
THAT'S WHAT'S MISSING.

$\mathcal{H}$APPY BIRTHDAY

—◄o►—

God has blessed you through these many
years,
through trials and tribulations and your many
ordeals.
But it's okay if I must say, God has a special
blessing coming
your way.

Out of all the good work that you've put in,
it's not in vain you'll
see it again.

Things you've said and encouraged me to do,
I found out later they
were also true.

God is going to bless you as you so deserve a
way of blessing where
you haven't seen or heard.

I just want to share God's love from up above
and share my love with a
great big hug.

SO I HOPE AND PRAY WHENEVER YOU
PRAY, THANK THE GOOD
LORD FOR THIS VERY SPECIAL
BIRTHDAY.

LOVE YOU ALWAYS.

$\mathcal{H}$ EAVEN

◄○►

If you are wise, I'd like to open your eyes to
the ties
of winning the prize,

where the truth lies, and lies dies, but to be
on God's
side, the truth you can't hide and you
definitely can't keep quiet
because you can't deny it.
"The truth is required."

God has prepared a perfect place for you and
for me,
it's located high in the heavenly, where eyes
can't see and
mortal bodies will not be.

There'll be no strangers, there'll be no danger,
everybody happy,
there'll be no anger, and we'll have wings, just
like God's angels.

We'll walk the streets, that's paved with gold,
there'll be no sickness
not even a common cold.
And everybody, we'll praise His holy name,
because we're different
we've been changed,
and that will remain.

enormous love all over the place, and there's
no such thing as "love at
waste," because there'll be "love to taste," love
at face and love so
great, until love won't have to wait.

$\mathcal{I}$ AM THAT I AM

◄◉►

I am He who most disagree, some want to be,
none can be,
I am He,
I am He, who will set you free, from all of
your sin and misery.
I am the stars, sun, and the moon,
believe Me when I tell you, my Son, Jesus,
will return soon.

I am weather, whether it's cold or whether it's
hot.
I'm the cause of you to have whatever it is
that you got;
I am rain, lightening and the thunder, I am
that I am so you don't
have to wonder.

I am your house, and I am your home, I am
your comfort, in your
heart is where I belong.
I am peace during a time of war, you can call
on me, I'm not far.
I am love that overtakes hate, I am that I am,
and I make no
mistakes.

I am the Spirit that you can't even see, I am to
bless you, but you don't
believe Me,
I am reproof, rebuke, I am that I am, I am
truth.

I am He who deserves all of your praise, so
don't get it twisted
because heaven and earth I made.
I am the Word in which I know you've heard,
and if you haven't
it's absurd
I am the air that you breathe, I'm more than
you want and all that
you need.
I am mind, body, soul, and heart, I am that I
am, I am God.

*I*T'S ALL ABOUT YOU

—◄◦►—

My Darling Dearest;

This I write, to suffice, what's right, because
what we have is tight,
and there's no darkness or night, just loving
light;
so this I've been trying and dying to say,
contemplating day after
day, so I choose today as your special day,
so you can have it your way, if that's okay.

I love your aggressiveness, progressiveness,
and when
we're not together, that I miss.
because you are the best, and I won't settle
for anyone less,
you've passed the test of real love and true
happiness,
together we're blessed;

you've been there for me when no one else
would or could,
you're very special and your heart is better
than good.
Not to mention your lips, strong fingertips,
just holding you
with a firm loving grip;

I'll never let you fall, nah! Not at all.
And being in our secluded space, nothing but
love all over our face,
and our conversation about God's mercy and
his grace;
never guessing, but caressing, and the
fluorescent of our bodies,
as we be undressing, we don't be messing but
flexing.

Yearning and turning, because our desires be
burning, and we be concerning
with one another learning.
Just you and I on a natural love high, you're
that jewel that I've found
to be true, it's not about me, but it's all about
you.

*I*T'S THAT TIME

◄○►

It's time, it's your time, brothers in the hood,
not understanding
life and time as they should or could,
I wish they would, so time would be better
than good. Let's stop
the crimes, where brothers and sisters are
unnecessarily dying,
mothers mourning at funerals, because it
wasn't their kids' time,
another brother is laid down forever, and we
don't know whether he's
bound for hell or heaven. But maybe you
didn't know it, but if you
live by the sword, you got to die by the sword.

And to sing that song, "The Sweet By-and-
By," remember the same
thing that makes us laugh, makes us cry.
It's time to be friends even with your foe,
because the Word says, you
reap just what you sow.
Everybody's drugging and mugging, forever
thugging and little
shorties plugging
nobody's hugging, and nobody's loving.
It's time, time to stop killing brothers and

sisters and let's start living
and giving and feeling, what the next man
felt, then we can play the hand
that we were dealt.

It's your time, it's gonna get greater later, if
you tell that madness, I'll
See you later,
because you're not a participator,
discriminator, and what they call a player
hater, you're here to be one of God's
motivators.
You know life can be whatever you want it to
be, it can be misery or a
mystery, but killing doesn't define your
destiny to prosperity.

Let's awake, right now on this date and make,
instead of the take of
(life) that's right we need a refreshing insight
on life.
And it's not about black or white, it's about
what's right.
So pass the word to those who haven't heard.

It's time, it's your time to stop the crime on
yours and mine, see time
and life is too short and with all the money in
the world, it can't be
bought, taught, or goes at naught. "Just a
thought."

So let's put it together, once and forever,
where it'll never affect us,
and we'll be better, regardless to whether...

Dig this, let's affect it!

*I*T'S YOU, LORD, THAT I NEED

—◄o►—

Lord, I pray this prayer, because I know You
care, I pray this
prayer, because I know You'll always be there.
When family and friends are gone their way,
You're never too
busy to hear me say, thank You, Lord, for
Your unlimited time,
because there's no one that gives divine peace
of mind.

I'm nowhere near perfection, and I make lots
of mistakes,
so I pray this prayer, that my sin be erased,
how ugly they
are before Your face, I plead my case by
mercy and grace.

I need Your help, because I can't help myself,
when I try and go
right, I end up left.
To You I can't lie, to You I won't even try, to
You I pray, Lord, please,
don't pass me by.
I've tried talking to people that I thought
understood, they would
laugh and smile, but meant me no good.
They would say things that made lots of
sense, but only to win my
confidence.

It was always "we or us" never once in God we
trust or in God
we must,
it's You that I believe, it's You that I've
received, it's You that I need,
and because of You, I'm relieved with the
assurance to do nothing but
succeed.

*J*ESUS PAID THE PRICE

—◄○►—

I know you think it's hard to live right for
God,
but that's not smart, just goes to show you
we're not
anchored in Jesus in our hearts.

With all the bitterness and strife, we need
right now, (To Repent)
and get it out of our life, and though you
wonder why your life
is dreary and weary and never serious,

you haven't been introduced to the helmet of
salvation and the
sword of the spirit.
And about that strife, it's been paid for twice,
because Jesus already
paid the price.
See, we need not God resist, but rather
submit, commit and don't quit,
because God's love is fullness.

It's going to be all right, because Jesus paid
the price, on Calvary He
died,
with two thieves on His side, "Remember

me," one replied and died
and him Jesus never denied, because he was
tied, so he set aside His
pride.

See, the enemy doesn't care, just want to
knock you off your spiritual
square, and leave you there, in great despair,
your inner man naked,

with nothing to wear, and that's not fair, it's
time to be aware.
Because when you're dead you're done, and
that's no fun then God
speaks, who hindered you son?

Well, you can't this time tell a lie, then God
commands His angels to
cast you into the lake of fire.

SO CHOOSE YOU THIS DAY, WHO YOU
WILL SERVE, THE
CHOICE SHOULD BE JESUS, HE'S WHOM
YOU DESERVE.

*J*UST A MAN

From the bottom to the top, Barack
we believe and we're not gonna stop, Barack.
A man that's been appointed, anointed, and
ordained for change.

A man that believe we can achieve, receive,
whatever we want, whatever we need.
A man that believe indeed, we will succeed
during crises like these.

A man that has a political plan, that will stand
and demand, and take us his people to the
promised land.
But he's "just a man," that promise, if given
that
chance, to promote peace, here, and in the
Middle East.

A man that believes together we stand divided
we
fall, but this was God's call for us all, yall!
Nov. 4, 2008, history was made and it was no
mistake, but great for this United States.

Barack Obama, "The Becomer," and yes he
can,
but let's not forget, "He's Just a Man."

$\mathcal{L}$IFE IS

Lives be crumbling and we be stumbling,
everyday wondering
and pondering.
Our ways of thinking have become nothing
but stinking, without
you even having an inkling.
We try and entertain, straight from the brain,
thoughts and faults,
that leave us in pain.
But whom should we blame for playing these
insane games?
Should these things remain or stay the same?
This God didn't ordain.
To choose and then lose, we become misused
tools, confused, our
pride bruised, with bad news, and corrupt
rules, we become fools.
See the game is to be sold and not told, but
for us it never unfolds,
and how it ends only God knows.
Short stakes and bad breaks, so when are we
gonna get a fair shake?
Where we can make instead of take, become
heavyweights and become
someone great, we need a break.
See we gotta survive to stay alive, away with
our pride, because they
got our hands tied.

With mouths to feed, they're selfish with
greed and we don't know who
to believe, so we stay in need and never
receive.
Politicians lying, keeping our people blind,
our kids dying, and we
don't see them until the next election time.
Now that's a crime that they pay no mind, but
it keeps us in the
welfare line.
Four or five churches on every corner, but to
help our people they
really don't wanna.
It's always, I'm gonna, we need donors, and
that's to keep up their
persona.
Now some was sent and others just went, so
watch the went, because
they haven't repent, and God knows they
weren't sent, and He's not
content, those are the people that God
resents.
So try and remember from January through
December, we won't
surrender, and we refuse to be hindered, so
we're moving on with our
daily agenda.
Then our start can begin, and everything else
will soon become an
end.
So we're wiping away our tears from present
and past years, because
that's the way life really is.

*L*OVING YOU

◄⊙►

You're the most lovable, incredible person on
God's green earth,
how I love you so much, until love begins to
hurt.

Sometimes we don't see eye to eye, things has
got to change,
and love is the reason why.

I think about you morning, noon and night,
that's right!
How can I forget, when we first met, you were
"all of that."
Polite, bright and I couldn't let you out of my
sight,
"you were my type."

I just want to keep our love right, because in
my heart there's
no maybe or might.

I play in my mind, you all the time, and that's
a good thing,
if you know what I mean, we're on the same
love team,
and the joy that it brings, it's reality, it's not a
dream,
as one makes it seem.

See I'm expressing, confessing, still learning
life's lessons, while others
be guessing, and messing, I be requesting for
God and all of his
blessings.

I'm very concerned, my mistakes, I've
learned, trying to live life on life's
terms.

See I'm a part of God, and these words come
straight from my heart.
Hoping and praying that our love don't
depart.

I hope you can see, that loving you like this is
all of me.
My love for you is so real and true, what else
is there for me to do?

JUST KEEP LOVING YOU.

$\mathcal{M}$Y BELOVED SISTER

—◄o►—

Out of all the women in this whole wide
world,
you're the one that I've considered my
favorite girl.
You're sensitive, caring, and to me very close,
your
heart and mind is what I feel the most.

God has blessed me with a sister like you,
we're one,
but yet we're two.
I just want to thank you for who you are, a
very special
sister whether we're near or far.

And the love that's implanted in both of our
hearts, we
won't allow nothing, I mean nothing, to tear it
apart.
I love you dearly, for who you are and for
what you've
done, you're my sister, and you're number
one.

I love you dearly, as in the beginning, because
genuine
love has no ending.

SO I HOPE AND PRAY THAT YOU DO
UNDERSTAND
YOU'RE VERY SPECIAL IN THIS MAN'S
LAND.

$\mathcal{M}$Y BETTER HALF

As the days turn into months and months
years,
the love that we have is truly God-sealed;
out of all the struggles that we've been
through,
I'm grateful to God, for someone that's
special as you.

Sometimes for me, life gets extremely hard,
but I wouldn't
couldn't give up because of you and God.
See, God has blessed us, with this beautiful
family, and I
myself, am thankful that you've chosen
someone like me.

You've shared hope and hospitality, and when
things were
right, you changed them quick, but very
polite;
even the moments of sadness or madness,
you were there to
support me with your time and much
gladness;

So I'll never hesitate to appreciate, the beauty
that God has
allowed us to create, I really want you to
know more than
words can express or even manifest, I LOVE
YOU, I LOVE YOU,
I LOVE YOU, this is from me to you.

Because there's no doubt in my heart you feel
the same way too.
And now that I think about it I can look back
and laugh, you're
So special to me, YOU'RE MY BETTER
HALF.

$\mathcal{P}$ROBLEMS

◄❍►

Problems, problems everywhere and there's
no one that
really cares, people say what they'll do, but in
the end the
play is on you.
So your mind starts thinking and your heart
starts sinking,
you get scared to death, now you thinking
about killing
yourself.
So you go to bed and say a prayer, but when
you awake the
problem is still there.
You go to your friends to see what they can
do, but they
can't help, they have the same problems as
you.
So now you find yourself where you first
began, lost with
no help, in a world of sin.
You walking 'round with your head hanging
down, mumbling
and grumbling some crazy sounds.

Problems, problems everywhere
and there's no one that really cares

So you think about your past and the way you
were raised,
mom and dad taught us to seek God's face.
Now is the time
to take their advice, to seek and to find the
Lord Jesus Christ.

Now all of a sudden you're a brand new man,
and people around
you just don't understand.
Whatever happened to the way you used to
be, they don't understand
you're god's holy and free.
So problems, problems they're all I've lost, I
gave to Jesus upon
His cross.

Taking your problems to Jesus Christ,
whatever is wrong, he'll
make it right.

REALITY

---◆◇◆---

Sometimes in life, things don't always seem
right,
but that's okay, tomorrow is another day.

We go through trials, to make us strong,
they're here
today and tomorrow they're lone gone.

It happens to everybody, so don't be alarmed
when trouble
comes, just know for yourself, why?
And where they came from.

God gives us inner strength to fight each and
every fight,
especially when nothing seems to go right.

See you're blessed by the best, and going
through a few things
is only a test that brings you closer to our
ultimate goals and success.
Life isn't always peaches and cream, and
everything that happens isn't
always what it seems.

So the more you know, the more you grow,
and the more you grow, the
more you got to know.

So keep your head up and reach for the sky,
because there's no limit
that you shouldn't try.

But keep in mind that life is designed, for us
to be unhappy and
troubled sometimes.

Because trouble doesn't last always and
forever and when it's over you'll
feel better than ever.

Reconciliation

For you, this I had to write, because you're
bright, you have great
insight, you're confident, there's no maybe or
might.

And your life is based on what's positive and
right, so don't be
surprised, that this poem for you is
personalized, and I now realized that my
heart can't keep quiet, "Forgive me for my
past;
I apologize."

I remember vividly, back in the days, when
you and I talked, I
should have mended my ways.

So here I am again, doing this later period,
acknowledging I miss
you, my darling dearest.
Not even dwelling on what happened back
then, hoping we can be
restored as friends.
I think, I know the woman that you are, we've
been distant, but
never too far.

If I were given the chance to do it all over
again, I would start with friendship
then romance, and watch love enhance, better
yet, "Just put me in a trance."

I'd be looking for love in its forever state,
maybe this long I've had to wait,
because waiting on you is never too late.
But nevertheless, allow me to confess, just
personally knowing you,
I feel that I'm blessed,

We have our struggles and troubles, but with
God in our life,
we must recover.

I understand, this you weren't anticipating,
but my way of communicating,
dictating, relating, never hating but, of
course,
reconciliation.

*S*ELF-EXPRESSED

–◄◊►–

My Dearest,
I'm sending you this, of course, and as you
read it, you'll be hearing
my voice.
Because these words of truth come straight
from the heart, this is
how I feel, and I mean the whole nine yards.

I tell myself time and time again, I'm more
than your lover, I'm
your very best friend.

And there's nothing I won't do for you,
because you're my Boo,
and what we have will never be through, and
I'm sorry
about my past rendezvous.

So I'm expressing myself, so I won't be by
myself, left, with bad health,
and being apologetic is God's heart felt.

So with your intellect, respect, and what we
have you and I, we will
protect, never neglect, forget, regret.

And it's not about being henpecked, just
caring much for you.

$\mathcal{T}$HE CHILD OF LIGHT

—◄○►—

This was a date that was set for birth,
nine months was total and we as family was
alert.
Then the time came for mom to conceive the
child "Child
of Light," the world would receive.

Brilliant and bright, and so well liked, entered
a world
so evil and impolite
the drugs, the gangs, stealing and killing all
these things
so true and revealing.
But after all that was said, seen, and done,
with God in
his life, the victory was already won.
He wouldn't associate, partake, participate,
cooperate,
collaborate, coordinate, He couldn't even
relate.

Now this is the "Child of Light" that would
not rebel,
and the Lord blessed him to do nothing but
excel.

Now his upbringing came from his mom and
sometimes
dad, respect and dignity, that's all he ever
had, so his life
was designed to shine, in yours and mine,
even in darkness,
during these perilous times.

THAT'S RIGHT, THIS IS THE "CHILD OF LIGHT."

$\mathcal{T}$HE LETTER FROM JESUS

—◄○►—

We were professing while you were gone, that
you'd learned
your lesson.
While the angels were protesting, that you
wouldn't be messing,
but expecting all your blessings, because of
confessing.
But once again you're playing the same old
game and that's because
you're free, the enemy got you blinded, and
you can't even see.
Remember the times when you and I talked,
and what you would do
if I let you walk.
How easy it is for you to forget, you owe me,
you're in My debt.
So next time I'm not hearing those lying lines,
"please let," "I'll
Respect," and I know you're disappointed and
upset.
But please don't let me go back on that deck.

I knew you were going to do what you did kid,
I knew your heart and
the light that darkness hid, but if you don't
change, I see a longer
bid.
You know every time you come home, you're

worse and worse, and you
really don't care who you hurt.
But that's okay, your family they'll be all
right, you're the one that's
going to suffer every day and every night.
And trying to be cool, thinking everybody's
your friend, watch
yourself, because you'll be needing me again.
And where will they be, during your time of
distress? doing the same
old mess, trying to impress, because that's
what they do best, not
caring less.
You're failing your test with that negativism
you possess.
Now some go to jail and others go to hell, but
if you're with me
both you will prevail.
Remember this, I choose you from your
mother's womb, I'm still
believing in you, so I'm giving you extra
room.

P.S. Get it together, I'll be back real soon
Love you Always,
Jesus

$\mathcal{T}$HE LETTER OF SINCERE

—◄◌►—

I've been admiring you for quite some time,
and I've adopted you
as a true friend of mine.
The way you carry yourself is so well
possessed, I feel that I know
you this I confess.
But nevertheless, I can't rest, because of your
inside-out beautiness.

I've made up my mind, that you will find, and
everything and everybody, I'll leave
behind, because you're my kind, and this isn't
some genuine line to blow your mind.

I'm serious and curious about having this
relation, with someone of your
reputation, which holds all the keys to
sensation and deep conversations, where
it's boggling my imagination, with frustration
and intimidation, and makes me
patient, where I'll have no explanation.

Can you understand, what I'm saying? Really
and truly I'm in demand. Can we
be more than friends?

I hope you'll take this straight to the heart,
and if you don't believe
me pray and ask God.

This I write not to defame you, but obtain
you, and to gain you
not to game you.

Your presence is here, when you are far and
near, I'm writing
you this because I'm very sincere.

𝒯HE LOVE OF A FATHER

—◀o▶—

It is often said time and time again, mom's
baby and dad's maybe.
One must know, show, and watch as fruit
grows.

Dad, you are the fruits for the many seasons,
and without your
producing there wouldn't be any reason.

My morals, values, and good qualities of life,
respect for others
without paying a price.

And though we struggle and you worked very
hard, our family of
course you wouldn't let fall apart.

So you are the king that caused great things,
and made me special,
a living human being.

So with your love and special care, these
words of understanding my
heart must share.

Dad, I love you today, tomorrow, and
forevermore, because loving you
dad, is love hard-core.

SINCERELY YOURS.

$\mathcal{T}$HE MAN OF GOD

◄○►

God gave me to you, that my life be complete
and true.

You were chosen from your mother's womb,
to teach

God's children that (Jesus) His Son is coming
soon.

He saved you, set you free, delivered and
added and

multiplied in your life.

Put you on the path of righteousness to teach
me, what

the Bible says is right.

He even from the world set you apart, and he
made you

a holy man, "A Holy Man of God."

Just like the shepherd watches over his sheep,
God has

given you the authority to watch over me (my
soul).

So keep on doing God's kingdom work, souls
are at stake

but we're not a mistake, just trying to relate.

So I encourage you in all of your doing, and
heaven I'll

follow you with all of my pursuing.

$\mathcal{T}$HE WAY WE WERE

Remember the times that we shared together,
love, joy, and happiness, they seem forever
and what the places that we used to go, then
all of a sudden we don't go anymore,

and how about the lovely words that was
often
said.
I think about them now, they blow my head,
yeah, the places we used to go, and the things
we used
to do.
It couldn't take one, it had to be two, but
that's a dream as real as it seems, we're still a
team.

And one thing for sure, the love, the time,
that we both
endured,

it wasn't just special it was supernatural and
pure.
However, I love you as in the beginning,
because
genuine love has no ending.

So what I found is so true, that's you,
love Unlimited.

To KILL, STEAL, AND DESTROY

◄◦►

My name is Satan, the prince of the air, I once
lived in heaven but I was
thrown out there;
and since that time, I've lost all of my joy, my
purpose now is to kill,
steal, and to destroy.
I have no respect for God, nor anything that
he has made, I'm after your
soul, then you're my forever slave.

I know your weakness, and I play just to win,
I'll slide beside you and
become your best friend,
and some of you are transparent, I can see
straight through, for material value,
for me anything you'll do

See, I've got you using and abusing God's holy
temple, with drugs, sex and war, it's just that
simple, I'm in your homes causing cussing
and fussing, but yet you're saying, "God is
whom I'm trusting."

I'm on your job each and every day causing
confusion because you don't even pray, and
even those that's high-minded, and full of
pride, many like that I've caused to commit
suicide.

Yeah, I see you when you're coming and
going, I'm all seeing and
sometimes I'm all knowing.
but Jesus is the answer, and you think He's
not, He died for you and that
was a lot, yet you think it's not.
I caused Moses not to make it to the promised
land, but not Jesus He has all powers in His
hands, and my desire is to sift you like wheat,
I have that power that you
can't defeat.

I COME TO KILL, STEAL, AND TO
DESTROY, MAN, WOMAN, GIRL, AND BOY.
MY NAME IS SATAN.

*T*O LIVE AGAIN

They say the game is cold, but it's fair,
I beg to differ with you because I've been there,
cocaine and heroin just to name two, I was caught up
knowing not what to do.

I had used and abused my body and not everybody,
being misused, I had to choose, refuse, defuse and this
time not lose,
see, my life was at stake, but I'm not a mistake, I'd hear
those voices about me making choices
(sources & resources).

This I had to make before it was too late, I was losing my soul,
my blood was cold, trying to carry this heavy load.
my mind and body was out of total control, from the lowest
to the poorest and I didn't even know it, I was about to blow it.
I was in a position that sent me on a mission (deadly), with no
nutrition.

A dope fiend with lost dreams, it was my time
to come clean.
So I cried out to God, "Help me, please!" This
I did on my bending knees.
I confessed my wrong and my sin, "Help me,
Jesus, to live again."
I know You can, and I hope You will, because
if you don't I can't
live.

Whatever it takes, Lord, I'm willing to do,
because life isn't life
if it's not with You.

He must have heard my call and He's seen my
cry, because deep
within I could live and not die.
Yeah, I suffered a little during my recovery
state, but after it was
over, I felt great.
My family was happy, and so was I, I could
once again live and
not die.

TORN APART

—◄o►—

My mind be drifting, heartbeat shifting,
could there be something that I've done
wrong.
I look back to exact the fact, whatever it was
it's now
gone.

I search from within to find the end, but it
has yet to begin.
So where do I start, with my mind or with my
heart?
Because I'm torn apart.

I do what I hate and hate what I do, but that's
the nature of me and you,
So I must pursue what I know to do, to
become true and of course being
new.

See, my life is not wasted, and death I cannot
taste it, so whatever it is,
I've got to face it.

My days are long and so are my nights, just
thinking of ways to make
life right.

I haven't lost, neither have I won, but I'm
going to with Jesus, God's
Son.

So forgive me, Lord, I pray from my heart,
because being
wrong I cannot dodge.

Help me, please, I pray of thee, that a worse
thing don't fall on me, I cry
out to you with a repenting heart, put it back
together, Lord, it's been
torn apart.

TRUE LOVE

◄◦►

I often wonder, how you and I met, we were
meant to be,
and I'm willing to bet;
I seek to find love, when it's fair, when I
found you, I found
love, true love there;
see, I was seeking for love in too many places,
and all the time
I was in the wrong faces;
they would tell a lie, to see me cry, without
knowing why;
anyway, one thing I've learned about true love
itself, it's endless,
everlasting, till the time of death;
but here's a promise that I'm going to make,
I'll be your friend,
your lover, just for true love sake;
spiritually, mentally, physically, I'll fight all of
your battles, just for
true love it really doesn't matter;
see, true love is the key to life's most
intelligent parts, it also opens
doors to equalized hearts;
true love has power that's holy and divine,
power that rules the heart
and the mind;
but understand this and do take notes, true
love is special that I need

most;
many lives are going up and down, reason
why, true love hasn't been
found;
true love is free and doesn't cost a stamp, and
can be everlasting if it
doesn't get damp;
last but not least, it's very much sweet, that's
inside out, life fresh
air, we can't do without.
True love is you, young, pretty and free, true
love is two people in love
not three;
true love is a gift from heaven up above,
perfect and upright, I'm
talking about true love true love.

$\mathcal{T}$RUTH OR CONSEQUENCE

—◄o►—

Listen, my sons, and do take part, daughters
are included,
because you're offspring of God.

Understanding your struggles in our unstable
life, but what I
don't understand is how you denounce the
Lord Jesus Christ.

God has allowed Him to be your personal
source, but unfortunately,
He allows you to make your own choice.

God understands your pain, your ill gain, my
God understands
everything.

But it's you that don't understand, so you're
doing your own thing,
not thinking about tomorrow and what it
might bring.

It appears to be forever, Satan makes it seem,
but it's your soul God
wants to redeem.

It's time to draw the line, body, soul and
mind, He's sitting on His throne
patiently waiting, while you're every day
contemplating,
procrastinating, debating, because with him
you're not relating.

It's now time to become yourself, you've
heard the word, so don't get left,
because you slept, it'll then be too late.

And nothing or no one can help, not even
fame or wealth.

Well, this I got to tell, this is not for sell, I'm
talking about the pits, the pits
of hell,

An existing place, not for you or me, it's a
place of darkness where
you have no identity.

There your soul will burn forever and ever,
and one day you'll get out,
and that day is called never.
So understand that the spirit of God doesn't
always strive with
man.

REPENT TODAY, WHILE YOU STILL CAN!

TURN OR BURN

True to salvation for the Kingdom is at hand.
(REPENT)
The Lord is coming with destruction in the
land.
Where will you be and what will you be doing
when
Christ returns and your life is all ruined?
Some of us think we have lots of time, but
obviously we
don't observe none of the signs.
People are killing every day, family and
friends that's
what the Bible says.
And look at the diseases, herpes and AIDS
that the poor
souls are getting from day to day.

The affliction of sex with one's sister or
brother, woman
and woman, man and man, today's
undercover lovers.
But think about Christ dying on the cross
saying, "Come
unto me all ye that are lost."

Now famine is another which the Lord has
revealed, showing
us today that His prophecies being fulfilled.

Beloved, this is no joke nor is it jive, make
haste, arise
be wise and realize.
And here you are waiting for the final
conclusion open and
blunt with no confusion.
See the essence of it all is being a brand new
man, accepting
the Lord and being born again, and there's no
fee that you must pay
except accept and believe and you're saved
today.
See when you believe, you receive God's spirit
so pure, there's
no doubt you're heaven bound for sure.
Your reservation has been made, your ticket
has been paid.

GRACE THROUGH FAITH ARE YE SAVED!

$\mathcal{W}$HY

—◆◇◆—

The minds of our blacks have deteriorated
away,
with no ethics, no plans for our future today.

We rob, we steal, or even kill our own
brothers,
neglecting, rejecting the thoughts of one's
fathers
or mothers.

But here's a brother saying let's increase the
peace,
sirens are screaming, eyes are gleaming,
another
brother is deceased.

So when will we learn? When will we turn?
After the effect, we've all been burned and
lost concern,
With no education, meditation, edification
and lots of
suffocation, with no location.
Wake up my brothers and remember the
dream,
Malcolm X, Marcus Garvey, and Martin
Luther King.

The dream is alive with no surprise, think
about it,
And you will arise.

So let's be wise and use our intellect, Hi-Tech
and be
respected...
So our children won't forget...forget...forget

Word Up, It's a Wake Up Call

I control your body and I control your mind,
I'll leave you handicapped with no lifeline.
I've got dealers using and selling,
I've got doctors, lawyers, and clergymen out there meddling.
I just play with your mind, I'm only blowing one more time,
but lying and denying, but slowly dying.
I'M THAT GIANT IN YOUR TIME.
Yeah, I'll let you blow and blow and then I'll let you know
that I can't let you go.
Because me and your body, we want some more,
remember, I'm the pimp and you're the whore.
And there's not one that stands toe to toe, or recognize you po,
at your very low, with no dough, you can't score, so a blow is a no no.
I'm in control of your body and your mind, I dictate your ills your body
chills.
I'M THAT GIANT IN YOUR TIME.
I'm the one that makes you commit violent crimes,
I'm in control of most pimps, players, and hustlers, I'll make your body

suffer, and your self-esteem less tougher and
if you try and ween away,
I'll get rougher, and begin to smother your
mother, brother, or any other,
that'll try to recover from these mad insane
troubles.
I control mood swings and other things, that's
why you're my dope-fiend
and it's going to cost much to become clean.
I'M JUST THAT MEAN.
I'm in control, I've made fools sell snowballs
to Eskimos, I won't allow
cross of a "T" or an "I" that you dot.
I'll tie your whole body in several severe
knots.
Talking 'bout Scotty got your body.
Well, I'm knotty, psychotic, erotic, takes your
wallet and your body,
and just when you think things are going to
be all right, I'll reach deep
within for a more expensive appetite.

BUT WORD! The only way out is Jesus
Christ, He's the reason why you
shouldn't pay the price.
He'll reconstruct, conduct, make it smooth
where it was rough,
he'll give you love and if that's not enough,
just say nope to that dope
And yes to Jesus, because He's that hope.

YOU AND I

A woman has a child, beautiful, smart with
radiance of God, smooth and
cool, obedient to mom's and some of God's
rules.
But all of a sudden you become rebellious, not
knowing that it leads
to Satan's earthly failures.

Yeah, I carried you for nine full months, not
behind, not on the side,
but right in front.

The food, clothing, and the shelter, heaven
knows, I've done my best, my child
you're taking it for granted, we've been
blessed.

See, God knows the truth, and how it'll set
your free, but what you're doing it's
against God and truly, it's against me.

See the world is full of lies, pride and alibis,
taking people for rides, after being
denied, and they still try it, some even admire
it.

But my heart is full of tears, fears, and over
the years unsealed to do God's will.

But you don't yield to what's happening in the
field, you think it's real until, you
live, then you give, and build, and get that
zeal to do God's will, then heaven
reveals from being concealed, then you
wonder, what's the deal, is it real?
IS IT REALLY REAL?

And a voice from within says, chill, chill, chill.
One more thing, showing the tools of life, an
instrument that shines in the night,
that's bright, that's a light, within your sight,
to help people fight for what's
right, whether it's black or whether it's white.

But I have only love to give, unconditional
love which is true and real, agape
love every day that I feel. Unchangeable love,
now that's God's love from
above.

Though I try and don't know why, maybe it's
about you, nah, it's
about You and I.

ABOUT THE AUTHOR

Mr. Rickey Quinn was born and raised in Indianola, Mississippi. He was brought up in the home of Mr. George and Cecilia Ann Quinn with hardcore discipline and a Bible-believing etiquette. He attended the best of public schools, Carver Elementary and Gentry High School, where he graduated and joined the U.S. Army.

But let's talk about the years of Rickey's growing up and how his life would down spiral, getting caught up in everything that was thought up. During his Christmas and summer vacations, he'd go to Chicago to visit his siblings. However, on one of those visits, he was recruited as a gang member, a Vice-Lord on the Westside of Chicago. He would then participated in basically any street activities that thugs participated in.

Rickey would steal, rob, commit burglaries and home invasions, and sell and use drugs, e.g., cocaine, heroin, PCP, until he became addicted, and his addiction would cause him to con people and pimp and play women for the love of their money. Living a glamourous thuggish life in and out of the Cook County Jail, his next destination was hell.

In 1984, Rickey was supposed to have gone south to visit his grandmother, which he would do every year for Thanksgiving. Because Rickey had a plan that would probably get him a lot of money, kidnapping was the motive to robbing a drug dealer. So on Thanksgiving morning, about 4:00 a.m., he was pulled over in a stolen vehicle. Rickey pulled off, and the high-speed chase began, speeds up to 100 mph in a residential community. He was later apprehended about 30 to 45 minutes and was in Chicago police custody. During the interrogation, he was beaten and tortured, but he never gave the police a statement, nor did he say a mumbling word. The next day, he was transferred to the Cook County Jail with a ransom for a $100,000 bond, with $10,000 to walk.

Rickey was stuck, and had to sit it out because the majority of his cases carried a maximum of 6 to 30 years in prison. He called his family, but to no avail. No one would come to his rescue, but they did get him a lawyer. Facing life and almost death, he was scared to death, so he began to put his faith in God and rely on Jesus. He began to pray and study his Bible, and the other gang-members joined him. Having rank in the organization, he had control over the other Vice-Lords, which was like being a supervisor on a job, and it was a job trying to govern everything and everybody on that deck (cell house).

Being a Vice-Lord, or a brother, you weren't supposed to eat swine or read the Bible. Vice-Lords honored the Holy Koran. Anything outside of that, you would be dealt with or violated, and Rickey was guilty again, this time with his own people. This time, he had a violation coming.

A meeting was called in one of the cells, and all the Vice-Lords were there to determine what his violation would be. But God knew that Rickey was serious about His Word and gave him favor with the brothers, and they decided to give him a pass. God saved him again; this time from a pumpkin head.

Rickey went back and forth to see the judge, who was a 99.9% conviction rate judge. After ten months of going back and forth, Rickey received God's favor, and mercy was also on his side. All of the class X cases were thrown out, and he pleaded, or copped out, for three years of probation and was then released. His charges stemmed from kidnapping to armed violence to attempted murder.

Again, God saved him, but he still hadn't learned. And, trying to be slick, he was locked up again. He didn't stay on the streets but 89 days and was this time charged with robbery, and the only thing that was going to beat him to the penitentiary was the bumpers on the bus. Right back in the cook county jail he was; this time he was gone. Rickey knew he couldn't beat the case, neither would he try, so he decided to get as much time in as he possibly could, then cop-out for the minimum sentence and go to the penitentiary. With six months in, he copped-out for three years and was home after 18 months.

Whatever it was to be learned in the penitentiary, Rickey learned and hasn't been back. But the county jail was always calling him as if his bed was waiting on him. He would get caught with heroin, because he became a junkie with junkie's habit, trying to sell but was his best customer. He would do 30 days here and 30 days there and the judge would throw the case out. His last case was when he had a pistol and drugs, somehow he got rid of the pistol but got caught with the heroin. Being locked up this time, he decided to analyze himself and agreed that the streets were killing him, and the next time might not be the jail but hell.

Being locked up, Rickey was diagnosed with high blood pressure, high cholesterol, congestive heart failure, and diabetes; you name it, he had it. So after getting out of jail this last time, he called it quits and has been straight since, due to the help of God and his lady friend who had used but has been clean for over 10 years. She has given her life to Christ, and God has been keeping her. She persuaded Rickey to do the same because she knew that the streets were going to kill him grave yard dead. He took her advice because he wanted to live and live the rest of his days with her and Jesus.

He asked for her hand in marriage, and she agreed. So the two of them have made a new transition from Chicago to Milwaukee, where they reside. Since they have been in Milwaukee, God has restored Rickey's faith in a full gospel Bible teaching church. He's now saved by the blood of Jesus, and he's a fulltime Christian, fighting a fulltime devil; but his victory is already won through Christ Jesus. Amen.

Rickey wants the world to know that if God be for you, He's more than the world against you. And like the songwriter says, "He saw the best in me when everyone else around me could only see the worst in me."

Printed in the United States
By Bookmasters